Praise for
Leading and Realizing Your Career Goals

"My fascination with Adesiji's approach to dealing with career *change*, *leadership*, and *mentorship* is in the fact that he shared with his readers challenges as well as practical approaches adopted to rise from a career stagnation. I can only describe this book as a 'read and do' and not a 'read and dream.' It's timely and a must read for many who are in search of practical as opposed to theoretical steps to a successful career."

—Jide Salu [Founder/CEO, 48Y Entertainment, Lagos, Nigeria]

"It would have been good for me to have had the opportunity to read this interesting piece by Adesiji about twenty-five years ago given that I went through a career without a mentor and learned a lot of the lessons through the school of hard knocks."

—David B. Wartman, CMC [Principal, Delta Strategy Group Ltd., Alberta, Canada]

"This book is an easy, enjoyable and informative read for anyone who wants to have a career rather than just a job. It combines proven common sense advice with thoughtful introspection to be both motivational and practical. Through his inspired writing Adesiji conveys a wealth of experience and a passion for his career, and the reader benefits from both!"

—Kendall Gibbons, MBA [Program Manager, Ontario, Canada]

Leading and Realizing Your Career Goals

Adesiji Rabiu

authorHOUSE®

AuthorHouse™
1663 Liberty Drive
Bloomington, IN 47403
www.authorhouse.com
Phone: 1-800-839-8640

Published by AuthorHouse 2/28/2013

ISBN: 978-1-4817-1549-2 (sc)
ISBN: 978-1-4817-1548-5 (e)

Library of Congress Control Number: 2013903582

Any people depicted in stock imagery provided by Thinkstock are models, and such images are being used for illustrative purposes only. Certain stock imagery © *Thinkstock.*

This book is printed on acid-free paper.

To my son, Tommy Rabiu, for prompting me to consider interests other than those that started this book. Thank you, son, for your insight and support.

May the eyes of your understanding be enlightened.

—Saint Paul

Table of Contents

Preface

Growing up, I remember being interested in a variety of different fields, including medicine and engineering. My friends and I had many interesting debates about which of us should pursue certain occupations—who should become a doctor, professor, engineer, or scientist.

In 1992, my professional path had begun, as I earned my first degree in computer science from the University of Lagos in Nigeria. For the next eight years, I explored careers as a high school mathematics teacher and as an IT network engineer and team lead for a technical services staff in the information technology industry.

By 2000, I had relocated to Canada. I landed my first job there with Siemens Canada, moving up the ranks to supervisor in Toronto. I collaborated with support groups in Texas and Munich to influence decisions that enabled the businesses of over 2,000 global customers.

In 2006, with over ten years of strong experience in the information technology sector, I moved west to Edmonton, Canada. The move prompted me to consider my long-term career goals and led to the development of a five-year "career changer" plan, which included earning an MBA and additional professional certifications in project management and management consulting.

By the end of 2011, while I had achieved an MBA from the University of Alberta and earned my project management professional (PMP) designation, I still had not obtained my last goal: the certified management professional (CMC) designation. Life had been happening while I was busy making plans and surpassing goals. Many unanticipated challenges, including job loss and six months of unemployment, had cropped up and interfered with my timeframe. As I write this near the close of 2012, I am on schedule to earn my CMC designation in the first quarter of 2013, albeit a year behind schedule. Even the best-laid plans need retooling to accommodate change. So what's next for my career? Read on!

Through what is contained in this book, I share about some of my learning experiences and the people and points of reference I've learned from. I also show the approaches I have created and adopted to manage my career choices and decisions.

In my experience, I've learned that having career conversations at work can be really challenging! Many workers are uncomfortable discussing career plans with their employers for reasons such as fear of unfair treatment and the risk of jeopardizing job security. It is important, however, for both job seekers and career changers to understand that many employers are receptive to and supportive of employees who are open, honest, and clear about their aspirations. Many employers appreciate employees who will make career adjustments that mutually benefit the employers and employees.

This book has been motivated primarily by a desire to document and share my personal experiences about making complex career choices and cultivating the determination to realize tough professional goals. Additionally, I want to introduce my son to the concepts of strategic thinking and decision making and share my experiences with family, friends, and others who face the perpetual challenge of making decisions.

Experience has taught me that taking the initiative to identify possible career options and mapping out clear paths to achieving the most suitable outcomes requires focus and strong commitment. Through perseverance and determined focus, success is an achievable reality, and this book will outline some key concepts for realizing your professional goals.

- Chapter 1 addresses perceptions and competencies. It explains how many people view career matters as well as some of the competencies required to manage a successful career.

- Chapter 2 shares some perspectives on self-monitoring—how, as individuals, we may influence or restrict our behaviors—as well as some perspectives on leadership and the competencies required to manage a successful career.

- Chapter 3 shares a framework for making career decisions. It explains crucial steps in identifying career options, managing the changes necessary for successful career transitions, and realizing defined career goals.

This book aims to support students, professionals, certified specialists, and lifelong learners who are challenged with making tough choices among a wide variety of career options. My intent is to incite strategic thinking and planful responses to achieve desired professional goals and outcomes.

This book, *Leading and Realizing Your Career Goals,* is written for anyone considering a career change or wondering, *What's next?* I encourage each and every one of you to pursue your career goals. By acquiring the right competencies and awareness, and through patience and persistence, any type of obstacle can be identified and subdued.

Many people never reach success—not because they are lacking talent or opportunity. They don't reach success because they are not tenacious; they just give up too quickly.

—*John C. Maxwell in* A Minute with Maxwell

Acknowledgments

Many thanks to Tommy Rabiu, Abolade and Gbolahan Adeyemi, Martins and Franca Orih, Afolabi Oguntade, and Olumide Olorode for their love and support.

I gratefully acknowledge all my friends, my colleagues, my learning partners at Leadership Edmonton, my mentors and protégés, and every person who has influenced my thoughts and decisions in one way or another.

Tracey Grozier and Balpreet Channey provided skillful editing and helpful suggestions, which I sincerely appreciate.

And as always, I thank God, who has inspired this work and enlightened the eyes of my understanding.

Chapter 1
Perceptions and Capacities

Developing and achieving an important goal requires and inspires patience, diligence, endurance, and fortitude. Doing what you love is one of the best gifts you can give yourself. And when you are solving problems or making choices, the ideal scenario is to have more than one option.

A good education, expertise in more than one profession, and the ability to harness engagement of multiple intelligences can be key enablers toward personal satisfaction in whatever career you choose to pursue. On the other hand, not having the right kind of education can stunt, stall, or even derail a career plan.

Planning for career success requires an understanding of some of the forces that impact perception and judgment and ultimately influence our actions. Before starting my MBA degree, I tried to anticipate a response to the number one question on most students' minds at some point in their academic careers: what job am I going to pursue after completing my studies? I needed to consider which position would provide me the right mix of challenges, personal development, and fair compensation, based on my acquired skills, experiences, and interests. I had decided to enroll in an

MBA program after ten years of industry experience, and that necessitated some reevaluation of the direction in which I saw my career heading.

Having a career presupposes that you have an ambition to persevere for many years in a chosen field of work or that you chose a profession with lifelong or long-term goals in mind. A job may be required, as a short term endeavor, to support your career goals.[1]

Perceptions

Perceptions and opinions held by others can delay your progress toward career plans and goals. In my experience, many colleagues have advised me against trusting anyone with my career plans. Others have told me the grass is greener on the other side, at another company. Time and experience have shown that this advice was not necessarily applicable to my own path. People are often biased by what has happened to them uniquely, so you should carefully examine advice before making decisions.

Here is my perspective, based on my experiences, about these two listed items of advice given to me by colleagues:

1. You cannot trust anyone with your career plans or goals.

As I mentioned in the preface, workplace conversations about career goals and aspirations can prove challenging, and at times, potentially polarizing. I've found that if you are working with an employer you respect, taking an open and honest approach to discussing your goals can lead to new opportunities. For many companies, employee retention and promotion from within are ideal outcomes, especially when there is the potential for growth that benefits both the employer and the goals of the employee.

---

[1]   In this instance, I am defining a job as a set of activities you perform in exchange for payment and which require fewer skills or less specialized training than those demanded in the average career.

2. The grass is greener on the other side, at another company.

In my experience, many people believe that to have the job satisfaction provided through increased responsibilities, more money, or upward mobility, you have to take a job at another company—that is, you may have to "move out to move up" or even move down to position yourself for opportunities. While this may be true sometimes, the notion of changing companies to feel more satisfied can demonstrate a myopic view in comparison to seeing the big picture. In addition, satisfaction with a new employer may be short lived.

I am currently employed by one of the best companies I have ever worked for. Staying, and taking advantage of the organizational knowledge I have acquired with this company presents me with fewer risks to manage and also allows me to leverage established relationships I've developed with people at different levels in the company.

I would suggest that the most important consideration to make before changing companies is whether your current employer can give you the kind of challenge or opportunity you're looking for. If your answer is yes, or even maybe, the next question to ask yourself is how to realize your desired career with this company. In my experience, I have always found that the best options come from within.

Capacities

In his book *On Becoming a Leader*, Warren G. Bennis states that a key competence for leaders is adaptive capacity. Effective leaders are also optimists; they are tenacious and demonstrate high capacity to adapt to change.

Knowing who you are and what you can do—your capacities—is fundamental to making wise choices. It is important to identify how your capacities relate to the limiting and enabling forces at play in your situation. This will help you not only to focus on what is important but also to develop capacities to position yourself strategically and handle challenges successfully.

Learning and Adaptive Capacity

There are diverse perspectives and opinions on learning as to where, what, when, and how we learn. There are always new skills and knowledge to acquire, and we can never know enough, but learning everything is simply not possible. Adaptive capacity encompasses not only one's ability to learn but also the ability to apply what has been learned to changing situations in the presence of various risks and uncertainties. The Action Studies Institute explores the nature of intelligent decisions, and I particularly like their description of the closely related concept of adaptive positioning:

> Adaptive positioning refers to the positioning of individuals in a dynamic field of threats and opportunities, their ability to identify and effectively respond to these threats and opportunities, and the process of adjusting their position and/or capacities, resources, priorities and responsibilities to lower the level of unmanaged or unseen threats and lost opportunities.

Literacy

Conventionally, literacy has been misconstrued as having the ability to read and write. If an individual were able to read and write but unable to think critically or acknowledge others' abilities, it would be unacceptable to label that person as fully literate.

The illiterate of the 21st century will not be those who cannot read and write, but those who cannot learn, unlearn, and relearn.

—Alvin Toffler

Today, literacy transcends reading and writing, and the term can suitably describe development of the capacity to learn how to reduce ignorance as well as apply knowledge and skills effectively. Namely, a literate person would demonstrate increasing proficiency in the following abilities:

- To read, understand, and appreciably apply knowledge

- To deduce and infer accurately

- To speak and converse intelligently

- To acknowledge and value others

Chapter 2
Perspectives on Leadership

Why do some people take the initiative to think and act? Why do others wait for people to think and decide for them? There may be several perspectives on ways to form an opinion. But generally we rely on ourselves, other people, or systems to control or determine who we are, how we are perceived, what or how we think, who we become, and even what careers we pursue. Censorship of ideas and information is a key factor.

Censorship

The censorship to which I am referring may be personal censorship—internally imposed by the individual—or cultural censorship that is externally imposed as a result of the environment in which the individual resides.

People encounter censorship in different ways—personally, culturally, or by other means such as the media, politics, or even the Internet, as shown in Figure 1. This requires career changers to be conscious of the factors and events happening around them. They must know what they want, what they can do for themselves, which professions are emerging, and which skills are required.

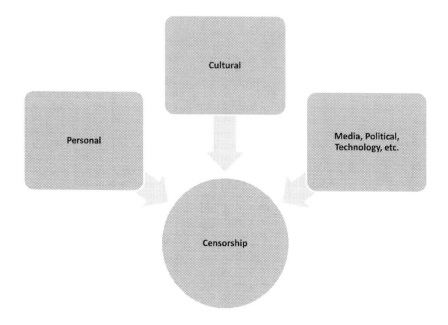

Figure 1. Understanding Censorship

Personal censorship is a form of internally or self-imposed restriction on the information one sees or thinks about. I've found that most people who ignore or overlook information are unaware of their situation and have done this unintentionally.

The other mentioned sources of censorship are externally imposed on the individual. Culture, in particular, is a form of external censor. Unlike personal censorship, which is motivated largely by ignorance or passivity, the ways that culture suppresses or obscures ideas and facts are more difficult to identify, detect, and overcome. This is because culture is rooted in a set of collective experiences, values, beliefs, expectations, and goals of a group of people within a certain system.

Overcoming personal and cultural censorship is essential—indeed, a prerequisite—to achieving personal goals, including those related to your career.

Ultimately, overcoming personal censorship is about gaining independence—independence from ignorance!

Leadership

I recently participated in a leadership program called Leadership Edmonton. I was challenged on multiple fronts and developed a more in-depth understanding of the concepts of wisdom and ignorance.

One takeaway for me was the distinction made that leadership does not have an "end state"—it is a journey! You learn to become a leader, and then you continue to develop and increase your capacity as a leader. The Leadership Edmonton perspective is well articulated in the description of "leader" provided by the Action Studies Institute, which facilitates the program:

> A leader is an increasingly resourceful, resilient, and responsible person with diagnostic and design capabilities for reducing ignorance and error, waste, suffering, and injustice at all levels, including individual, community, national, global, and spanning entire civilization.

Over the course of my career, I have learned that development of one's leadership is continuous and does not have an end state. A leader is a person with diagnostic and conceptual capabilities for solving problems in innovative and resourceful ways.

When I think about leadership, I consider three specific types: personal leadership, decision leadership, and change leadership, as described in Figure 2.

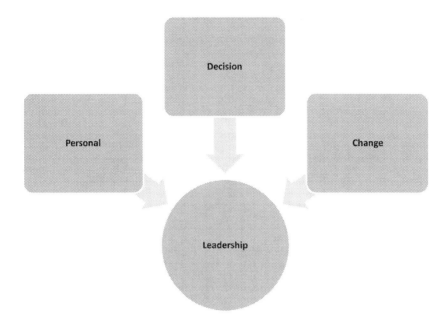

Figure 2. Types of Leadership

Personal Leadership

Many leadership conversations and commentaries have centered on personal leadership. It is often identified as the most important of the core pillars of leadership.

Personal leadership refers to leading oneself. It is about having self-control and self-management—the ability to positively influence our own emotions, thoughts, and actions. Other attributes of personal leadership include being able to express our thoughts and feelings appropriately, possessing a good measure of energy and capacity to endure challenges, and being patient and tenacious—shaping one's character and conduct with limitless patience, goodwill, and desire to learn. As US President John F. Kennedy stated, "Leadership and learning are indispensable to each other."

Leadership is a lifelong task, and effective leaders are eager to learn new things. They are aware of their values, beliefs, and expectations; they are willing to make necessary attitude changes and unlearn unproductive habits to be more effective. Successfully leading oneself involves identifying those whom one can learn from and engaging them in a rewarding protégé-mentor relationship. Having the right mentor may provide several benefits such as career advancements, enhanced development of leadership capabilities, and expansion of professional networks.

Some important personal leadership qualities and traits are professionalism, integrity, working safely, skillfulness, trustworthiness, and understanding and respecting the needs of others. Having a grasp of social and emotional intelligence is also important.

Decision Leadership

How can we ensure that our performance in our chosen endeavors is optimal? One good step is to carefully consider all relevant forces at play before making decisions. Another is to see to it that all subsequent actions are deliberate, intentional, and outcome based. These are aspects of decision leadership as we guide ourselves or others in effective decision making.

Mastering decision leadership involves developing diagnostic and conceptual capacities as well as a deep understanding of the relevant forces impacting any given scenario ("forces" are examined in the next chapter).

Utilizing the behaviors of generally effective leaders can help a person to be a decision leader in particular. According to Michael E. Porter, a strategy guru from Harvard University, "The essence of strategy is choosing what not to do." Similarly, decision leadership is about doing the proverbial "right things" and identifying what not to do. Effective leaders identify and evaluate problems, develop the right frame for generating and executing solutions, consider options and opportunities, and then make sound decisions, but only after thorough consideration and understanding of the underlying forces.

Effective leaders learn to manage the consequences of the decisions they make. In order to do this effectively, leaders continuously update and improve decisions as new information become available. In this process, they also continue to develop higher-level understanding about their own thinking and inquiries.

Each person—including every career changer—can imbibe these attributes of effective leaders and learn to make sound decisions.

A good decision is like "quality" as described by William A. Foster: "Quality is never an accident; it is always the result of high intention, sincere effort, intelligent direction and skillful execution; it represents the wise choice of many alternatives."

Change Leadership

Leaders who make quality decisions tend to have a good measure of personal and change leadership. Change leadership is a more complex concept with several crucial components. The focus of change here is not on managing organizational change. It is on managing personal change—one's own change—especially potentially unproductive habits that may impact career goals. The leadership component of change leadership refers to coordinating or guiding change about oneself or others as well as to leading by example.

Change leadership is becoming more and more prevalent in modern society with the mounting pressure to constantly adapt. Many people seek to avoid change, because they lack the skills to cope—most often as a result of not knowing how future outcomes will manifest or will impact them. Some people are apprehensive that change may result in loss of control over what they already have. In other cases, those in the midst of change are simply unreceptive to uncertainties, especially as they transition between their current state and desired state.

A few years ago, as part of my professional development, I took a change management course through the Canada Association of Management Consultants. Some of my learning and personal experiences are articulated as a perspective on change leadership in Figure 3.

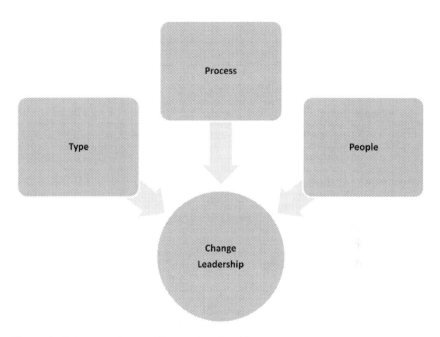

Figure 3. A Perspective on Change Leadership

Types of Change

Change can be divided into two broad categories: developmental and transformational.

Developmental Change

Change that is developmental is geared toward personal improvement—including performance enhancements and problem solving—without changing one's mindset or acquiring new values. Personal values are usually retained, but there is increased awareness of an "ignorant space" and the need to fill that space with new knowledge.

Developmental change is relatively simple, and it typically is fairly inexpensive in terms of personal resources (time, effort, and money) required to achieve it. An example of developmental change is the acquiring of new or advanced skills to function in a more senior position in your current job group.

Transformational Change

Change that is transformational requires a shift in mindset, which in my experience has proven necessary to survive or thrive in competitive domains. External forces, such as recession or employer downsizing, may trigger transformational change. At other times, someone who is learning new values and has developed other interests undertakes it proactively and purposefully.

In an organization, for example, transformational change is often required to address issues associated with culture. Similarly, it is often necessary for correcting habits and behaviors in individuals.

Compared with developmental change, which is relatively easier to achieve, transformational change is usually more challenging and may involve the support of external parties or influences such as mentors or coaches. It is also typically more expensive in terms of personal resources.

To illustrate this: After more than ten years of working in the information technology industry, I decided to go back to school to earn an MBA degree. I was very interested in the electricity business—generation, transmission, and distribution—but upon graduating after twenty months of spending and rigorous study, I did not find a suitable position with a power company. I had obtained my MBA degree just at the start of the recent global recession, which had significant negative impact on my target industries; my managing of the required transition was extremely challenging.

In order to overcome my challenge, I reached out and developed new mentorship relationships, I continued to enhance and relearn skills, I continued to work wisely and diligently, and I remained optimistic. Yes, transformational change may include acquiring new or advanced skills to function in a new job that is different from what you are used to doing or requires a different level of competence. However, while I enjoy what I do now, I am still able to leverage my residual knowledge, skills, and competencies as I work toward interests in business development, project leadership, and leadership development. The challenges I overcame helped me to develop new interests and capabilities. Simply stated, I am more versatile, more resilient, wiser, and less ignorant.

Process of Change

Effectively leading change requires articulating the case for change—the reason why you want the change and the desired outcome—and identifying personal readiness. Regardless of the type of change taking place, the process of change is consistent with endings, transitions, and new beginnings, as described by transitions expert William Bridges.[2]

---

[2] William Bridges, *Managing Transitions: Making the Most of Change* (Boston, MA: Addison-Wesley, 1997).

Endings—These involve letting go of your old or current state. Holding on to old ways of doing things, old ideas, or old unproductive habits will not support seamless transition to your desired state.

Transitions—This term describes the gap, and especially the experience, between the old state and the new or desired state. You are learning new things and habits in this state and unlearning old ones; looking back often and anchoring to the past will hinder progress toward a desired or new state.

New Beginnings—These are influenced largely by your vision and objectives. You know you have entered this phase when you have fully embraced the challenges you must overcome to be successful. You are no longer looking back, but are focused on identifying opportunities that will enhance your competence and increase your confidence in achieving your short (intermediate) and long term goals.

Having a good idea of where you are in your change experience will help you to manage both the change and the desired outcomes more successfully.

People in the Change

When you consider organizational change, it is important to have champions and agents who sponsor and promote the change required. In personal change leadership, the protagonist and change agent is you. You may also require support from other people—perhaps your mentors, or in other cases, your protégés or peers—in order to achieve desired outcomes.

Do not hesitate to ask for help if you feel you need some. You and those who support you will be able to endure the endings, transitions, and new beginnings that change entails with fewer challenges, provided you have engaged the right people and support.

During the process of change, you need to be conscious of how you feel about the requirements for successful transitions, and how involved and accepting you are of these requirements—I use the acronym EIA as a prompt to monitor my *emotions*, *involvement*, and *acceptance*. Similarly, you need to monitor the EIA of each person you have engaged to support you. The level of commitment and support you receive from each person should accord with predetermined mutual expectations. Also, you must continually monitor, evaluate, and update your approach for pursuing and realizing your desired outcomes.

Change is inevitable. The change we need should be pursued proactively; otherwise it may be imposed on us, either directly, such as when we lose a job, or indirectly, such as when we are no longer challenged in our current role. Effective change leadership is essential for realizing your desired career outcomes.

You may have developed capacities to lead yourself effectively and the competencies to adapt to change and make effective decisions, but leading and influencing others can be a totally different experience ...

- *the one who is led reserves the right of followership!*

- *the decision whether to follow you is theirs!*

Chapter 3
Career Decisions

The preceding chapters shared fundamental information about identifying and achieving desired career options through making effective decisions.

Developing and achieving a desired career requires patience, diligence, endurance, and fortitude—and it can inspire these qualities as well.

> We cannot become what we need to be by remaining what we are.
>
> —*Max DePree, former CEO of Herman Miller*

Career decisions and conversations cannot be taken lightly, since they have the potential to impact many important aspects of our lives. In the pages that follow, I will share the method that I am using to inform my career decisions. I will also address the challenges I have faced on my path to achieving career goals. Let's begin by looking at the Framework for Career Strategy.

Framework for Career Strategy

The Framework for Career Strategy is designed to help inform your thinking, support evaluation of your personal worth, and identify and articulate your preferred career options and goals. This model represents a feasible strategy by which to realize your desired outcomes through effective decisions and intelligent actions.

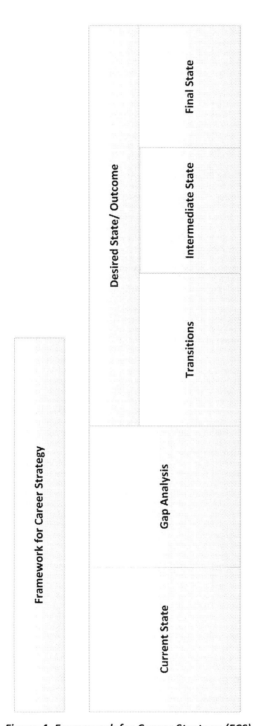

Figure 4. Framework for Career Strategy (FCS)

The Framework for Career Strategy provides a comprehensive method for self-discovery. It consists of three parts. The first two parts will help articulate your current state and your desired state or outcome. The third addresses everything in between those two points that supports the identification of potential interim options and final career destinations. These concepts become clearer in using the more detailed version of the Framework diagram in Figure 5.

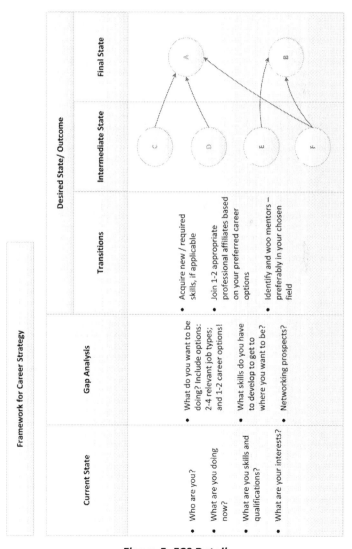

Figure 5. FCS Detail

Current State

Answering the key questions in this state will help you to articulate your identity and interests and to develop a well-informed gap analysis. This should include identifying your strengths, weaknesses, opportunities, and threats. Additionally, by the time you answer these questions, you will be able to provide additional relevant input to your resume. In my case, I would respond to the Current State questions as follows:

Who are you?
- An outcomes-based performer and a critical thinker with a quick grasp of sophisticated tools, technologies, and environmental scenarios; a strategist, change leader, and decision leader; a competent provider and implementer of innovative value-adding solutions and recommendations.

What are you doing now?
- I am a leader in a project management office, with accountabilities for the collaborative definition, governance, and enforcement of project management standards.

What are your skills and qualifications?
- Management consulting, strategic project and portfolio management, change and decision leadership, coaching, and mentoring.

What are your interests?
- Strategic project leadership, business development, and human resources (particularly leadership development).

By the time you document your current state, you will have developed more clarity and understanding of how well your current position is aligned with your interests.

Gap Analysis

The Gap Analysis stage focuses on identifying the steps to take in moving from the current state to the desired state. (Gap analysis is a tool commonly used in various business contexts.) The key questions to address here include the following:

- What do you have to do to make the future that you desire come to fruition?

- A prerequisite to this is doing some thinking to identify possible future states—at least two potential future states, one primary and the other secondary, with either providing a satisfactory level of achievement.

- What skills do you have to develop that will support your decision?

- Should you enhance existing skills?

- Should you acquire new skills?

- Would it help to join a professional association—perhaps one that supports or regulates your desired career profession? In most cases, affiliation with an association will highlight your interest and may provide valuable networking opportunities.

The Gap Analysis phase is an essential part of the Framework for Career Strategy. You should meticulously and diligently answer the questions posed above. While thinking about your unique situation, you might also have to answer other questions, such as where your choice career should be located—Calgary, Houston, Abuja, Accra, London?

Articulating the forces at play in your unique situation will help you determine where to invest your efforts and resources. At a minimum, you should consider addressing those suggested in the career progress "force fields" outlined later in Figure 6.

Desired State/Outcome

The state called "Desired State/Outcome" is also referred to as the future state. It is extremely important to articulate what this state consists of in your case, since you will have no direction or ability to monitor progress if this state is not well articulated and defined. The desired state includes three sub-states: transitions, intermediate state, and final state, as noted in Figures 4 and 5.

Transitions

Transition periods may be very challenging. During this period, many changes required for success can fail, for many reasons that include ignorance, lack of discipline, inflexibility, and inability to adapt. Transitions may last a few months, but in many cases they can last several months or years.

During transitions, you are learning, you are focused, and you have your desired outcome in mind. It may be the time when you are acquiring new skills, developing new relationships, or enhancing current skills to prepare for the next big opportunity or challenge. In this period, you should also consider joining any relevant professional associations related to your desired profession. Find out if your target profession requires professional certification, and start working toward achieving such certifications.

Finally, this is an excellent time to identify and woo mentors in your chosen field for guidance and encouragement. Think, look, search, and you will identify a suitable person—either in your primary or secondary career area.

Intermediate State

Often, transitions occur alongside intermediate states. During the intermediate state, you are still in transition and on your journey to your desired outcome. If you invested a good measure of time and effort in the Gap Analysis stage, there will be a few relevant career options for you to consider as potential intermediate states, which are indicated by bubbles C, D, E, and F in Figure 5.

Although the name suggests an interim state, do not be surprised if you realize that you are comfortable enough to remain in the intermediate state for a time, as you may find similarities between career options defined in the intermediate and final stages. This may result in situations where you have completed the tasks of the Gap Analysis stage with rigor and diligence and where a few potential options have been identified.

Final State

In the final state, you have narrowed your exploration down to one or two career options. It is expected that either of these two options will provide you with long-lasting engagement and satisfaction. However, because our wants are often inherently insatiable, it would also be normal if your values change after a few years and you start thinking about a change, perhaps a change to your identified alternate career option or to one of those identified in the intermediate state.

The key is to do what gives you the most meaning and satisfaction. Be sensitive to the needs of your employer, and be flexible if new forces emerge in your domain—be adaptive and take intelligent actions that will lead you and guide sustained progress.

Forces that Drive and Oppose

Forces are another crucial component in planning career directions. It is essential to clearly articulate what is motivating your desire to want "better" or "best" and to want to change your career—what is inspiring you? These motivations are generally referred to as the driving forces. Counteracting the driving forces are impediments—things that may stall or derail progress as you work toward your desired future states. These are referred to as opposing forces, as outlined in Figure 6.

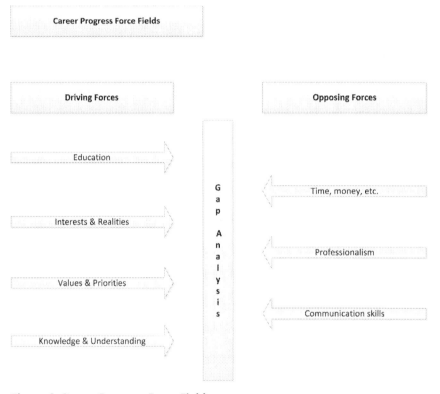

Figure 6. Career Progress Force Fields

Success in achieving your desired future state is greatly enhanced through diligence and clear understanding of all relevant driving and opposing forces at play in your unique situation. Properly aligning and managing them through wise decisions and intelligent actions will help you reach your desired final state.

Driving Forces

Education: What education and experience do you have? Do you have the right education to support achieving your desired outcomes?

Interests and Realities: What are your interests? What is achievable? Separating assumptions from facts will enable you to articulate what is real, reasonable, and accomplishable.

Values and Priorities: What are your values? How do they influence your interests? In the event there are multiple options, how would you align them to your interests and determine which ones comes first—how do you prioritize? Where do you expend your current resources in order to derive the greatest benefit?

Knowledge and Understanding: How much understanding do you have regarding your desires and current challenges? What are you ignorant about, how will you get the information you need, and where do you need to focus your attention concerning your desired career?

Opposing Forces

Time, Money and Life Stressors: How busy you are in your current career and life situation may impose time constraints that limit how much you can do. For example, if your family has a single income, finances might be an issue that impacts the pursuit of certain goals. You may have to be resourceful to save as much as possible, or deprive yourself of enjoying some luxuries in the meantime, but delayed gratification can be more beneficial to you in the long run.

Professionalism: This describes the competencies and capabilities expected of a professional. It is one thing to secure a job; it is a totally different story to sustain your interest and performance and keep your job. Professionalism begs for answers to questions such as these:

- Are you flexible?

- Can you talk and work with people you are not fond of?

- Do you show commitment to quality?

- Do you take initiative, identify challenges, and acquire the knowledge and skills to resolve them?

    Lacking professionalism is a major impediment to achieving success in any chosen career, even in those where you possess domain expertise. A professional will be motivated to do only ethical things, personal or otherwise, in order to get the job done. Typical attributes of a professional will include these:

- Trustworthiness, accountability, and integrity

- Open and frank communication and the ability to debate openly

- Social responsibility

- Courage and respect

- Inquisitive disposition and ability to take initiative

- Innovation and flexibility

- Reliability, collaborative manner, and results orientation

Communication Skills: Effective communication is achieved through more than speaking clearly. It includes listening and paying attention to what is being communicated to you. When you combine speaking clearly and listening effectively with positive body language and facial expressions, you can effectively influence the people around you. Applying good communication skills will support you in these matters:

- Articulating accomplishments, skills, and competencies and relating them appropriately to your future state

- Explaining relevant experiences and examples and sharing what you learned as a result of these experiences

- Articulating your thoughts and asking well-developed questions

- Demonstrating unwavering commitment to your defined career goals

    Depending on your background and interests, transitions may take a few months or even several years. Note that taking a long time to arrive at the final state is not necessarily a bad thing!

    In fact, in my case, the duration of my transition period—still ongoing—has provided opportunities to learn more, enabling me to

- *develop an unusual depth of knowledge in diverse areas;*

- *build character and a temperament that is more patient, tenacious, collaborative, and creative; and*

- *enhance my ability to succeed in any chosen career.*

Conclusion
Commitment to Action

During a church service I attended in Lagos, the preacher spoke a thought that really resonated with me: "You need to disable all excuses."

So what is holding you back? Whatever your excuses for not moving forward, disable them. *You need to disable all excuses!* Now is the time to act—to start executing the plans and taking the steps you have been considering since you began reading this book. Taking the initiative and responsibility to identify possible career options and mapping out clear paths to achieving the most appropriate outcomes will require discipline and strong commitment in making decisions and taking wise actions.

The table below shows decision domains you may traverse, as well as recommended tools to use, while developing understanding, actionable alternatives, and a path to progress toward your desired career outcomes.

Decision Domains		
Domain	**Tools & Measures**	**Comments**
• States	• "Define" current state & future state	
• Diagnostic	• "Perform" force field analysis, Gap analysis	
• Creative and Innovative	• "Generate doable" options	
• Execution and Transitions	• "Identify and take" interim assignments, training, professional development/ affiliates	• **Decision Domains** (states, diagnostic, creative & innovative, and execution & transitions) identify the phases that will be traversed as based on the Framework for Career Strategy

Figure 7. Decision Domains

Go out, meet new people, and build a reliable network. As you consider identifying and wooing mentors, remember that there are those who also look up to you.

Winning and achieving success are contingent on flexibility and on building a character and disposition that reflects patience, tenacity, collaboration, and creativity. By acquiring the right sets of skills and awareness, and through diligence and persistence, any type of obstacle can be identified, clearly articulated, and subdued.

Delay no further; now, get to work—you cannot realize a goal you never pursued!

Your development, and perhaps success, may depend on how receptive you are to helping and supporting the goals and aspirations of others.

While it might be reasonable and expected to set hard timelines on most initiatives or projects, it may be unreasonable to do so with a projected career change.

Remembering the words of John C. Maxwell, so many people fail to achieve success because they lack the persistence, not the ability or opportunity, to get the job done. Don't let this be your fate!

References

Baggett, Byrd. *Dare to Lead: Proven Principles of Effective Leadership.* Nashville, TN: Cumberland House Publishing, 2004.

Bennis, Warren G. *On Becoming a Leader.* Cambridge, MA: Perseus Publishers, 2003.

Bridges, William. *Managing Transitions: Making the Most of Change.* Boston, MA: Addison-Wesley, 1997.

Buckingham, Marcus, and Coffman, Curt. *First, Break All the Rules: What the World's Greatest Managers Do Differently.* New York: Simon & Schuster, 1999.

Clawson, James G. *Level Three Leadership: Getting below the Surface.* Upper Saddle River, NJ: Pearson/Prentice Hall, 2009.

John Maxwell Team. *A Minute with Maxwell* video message, accessed at http://www.johnmaxwellteam.com.

Lundin, Stephen, Paul, Harry, and Christensen, John. *Fish!: A Proven Way to Boost Morale and Improve Results.* New York: Hyperion Books, 2000.

Maxwell, John C. *Developing the Leader within You.* Nashville, TN: Thomas Nelson, 2005.

About the Author

Adesiji Rabiu has over eighteen years of combined experience in IT, project management, and management consulting in both private and public sectors. During the course of his developing career, he has held positions such as high school teacher, network engineer, senior product support analyst, researcher, regulatory analyst, strategic planner, senior management consultant, management consulting specialist, and project management specialist at companies including ICL–Fujitsu, Resourcery Limited, Siemens Enterprise Communications, Natural Resources Canada, Alberta Utilities Commission, and Enbridge Pipelines Inc.

Adesiji's training and professional development have taken him to the United Kingdom, South Africa, the United States, Germany, France, Belgium, and the Netherlands. Adesiji enjoys problem solving, debating, and pursuing lifelong learning opportunities. His specialties and interests include the following:

- Management consulting

- Strategic project and portfolio management

- Change and decision leadership

- Coaching and mentoring

- IT strategic planning

Adesiji is currently on the board of directors for the Institute of Certified Management Consultants of Alberta, and he has served on the board of directors for the Project Management Institute—Northern Alberta Chapter.

In addition to this publication, Adesiji has authored *The Cost of Electricity in Nigeria,* published by the International Association for Energy Economics (IAEE).

Adesiji holds a master of business administration degree from the University of Alberta, an advanced certificate in project management from Stanford University, and a bachelor of science degree in computer science from the University of Lagos in Nigeria.

Adesiji resides in Edmonton, Alberta.

Printed in the United States
By Bookmasters